NANNY SAYS

NANNY SAYS

as recalled by

SIR HUGH CASSON

and

JOYCE GRENFELL

edited by

DIANA, LADY AVEBURY

SOUVENIR PRESS

First published 1972 by Dobson Books Ltd.
This edition published 1987 by Souvenir Press Ltd
43 Great Russell Street, London WC1B 3PA
and simultaneously in Canada

'Nanny' by Virginia Graham from *Consider the Years*
is reproduced by permission of *Punch* and the author.
Extracts from *A Late Beginner* by Priscilla Napier
(copyright © 1966 by Priscilla Napier) are reprinted
by kind permission of Curtis Brown.

Apologies are offered to any author plagiarized
by Nanny.

ISBN 0 285 62826 7

Typeset, printed and bound in Great Britain by
William Clowes Limited, Beccles and London.

DEDICATION

*To all nannies and ex-children –
particularly those who have
contributed to this book.*

FOREWORD

There now . . .

It is fashionable to decry old style nannies and there is reason for some of the criticism levelled against them. In London, when I was a child, Hyde Park nannies were very grand indeed. Their standards of the outward and visible were high; their values seem less reliable, but then, they took colour from those who employed them. There was much competition about the social position and possessions of their Bosses; over the glossiness of their prams – some bore coats of arms – and about their charges' clothes. Some Hyde Park nannies bullied their nursery maids and sapped the exploratory instincts of the children they looked after by keeping them close and forbidding games and adventures that might result in excitement, heat and dirt. Bold spirits were soon quenched: 'Just look at your hands – and your knees. What will people think'.

Those of us who moved in less lofty circles, and have known the comfort and joy of being cared for by the kind of nanny I had, will join me in singing praises and giving thanks. The kind of nanny I salute may not have read many books but she was wise, steady and to be relied on for the unchanging certainty of selfless love. I now realise my nanny was a socialist as well as a royalist and

Non-conformist. She also had a slightly shame-faced faith in what the tea leaves revealed. Above all she was good as gold, strong and gentle. She had no formal training but had learned by doing, first at home, where she helped to look after the younger children, then at fourteen as a nursery maid under an established nanny. Finally, when she was twenty-one, she left to take on her first baby 'from the month' and turned into a nanny herself. I was her first baby 'from the month' and we loved each other from the day we met until the day she died, fifty-three years later.

All the nannies in my era seem to have conformed to an unwritten law that they should wear grey coats and skirts, white cotton blouses, sensible black shoes, sensible black hats and grey cotton gloves. They wore starched white aprons in the nursery and voluminous flannel ones at bath time. My nanny had a silver brooch called MIZPAH made of clasped hands. She had a white buckram belt that fastened with an interlocking silver buckle and when she bent down to kiss me goodnight there was the interesting creak of whalebone to be heard.

There were other sounds special to the nursery: the click of a needle pricking through cambric followed by the faint hiss of cotton being drawn tight; the particular plop-plop nanny made as she tested the temperature of my bath water with her elbow and said: 'There now.' She said 'There now' a good deal. After she had buttoned my blunt-toed shoes she patted the soles, removed me from her lap and said, 'There now, down you get.'

Unlike most mothers today nannies only led one life at a time and that life was fully dedicated to the nursery where a familiar repeat-pattern of days, as well as responses, made the climate a good one to grow roots in. One gained confidence enough to take on wider adventuring when the time came for it and in my case, I was encouraged to be independent. There was no maternal 'smother-love' loving in our kind of nursery; common sense and kindness prevailed. Successful nannies were not over protective, for they knew the world could be a rough place and their job was to equip us so we could get along in it. They also knew that encouragement helps.

'Not bad, all things considered.'

'Now you can do better next time.'

'It's silly to say you can't – of course you can – you'll manage.'

So you did a bit better, and managed. One marvels now at the patience and enduring good temper of nannies bombarded by repeated 'why's?' The answers were not always satisfying:

'Because I say so.'

'Don't ask silly questions, dear.'

'But, Nanny . . .?'

'But me no buts.'

Little bits of nanny-wisdom have stayed with me for ever. I still 'undo' my coat when I go into a warm atmosphere so that I may 'feel the benefit later'. At tea I still 'start plain and finish sweet' and when I am tempted to eat in a rush I can still hear that quiet voice saying – 'Don't bolt, ducky, eat sensibly.'

In her book *A Late Beginner* Priscilla Napier has a good ear for nanny murmurings. She lived in Egypt until she was eight. She and her nanny had been to look at the Pyramids.

'What are they for, Nanny?'

'Tombs, dear . . . Where's your other sock?'

'Who put them there?'

'The Pharoahs did . . .'

'Waiting for the Last Trump?'

'Yes,' Nanny said knowing better than to hestitate. 'Your other sock is in the doll's bed and that it got there by itself I beg to doubt.'

Priscilla Napier also pin points nanny's insularity:

'Cress!' Nanny said, 'In *France*. The very idea!' and, later, 'You should know better than to lose your temper in front of foreigners.'

Another nanny in another context was taken to see the great windows in Chartres Cathedral. 'It's a very dim light to sew by,' she said.

This book is a collection of what Virginia Graham calls 'The strange, comforting, senseless things' nannies used to say when I was small. They seem to be reflexes rather than thoughts, echoes of other voices long since silenced. Nanny-talk invokes for me the firmness of a loving hand with a hair brush, a face flannel and buttons. 'There now.' I remember red coal fires and the pleasant smell of vests airing on the nursery fire guard; the click of a clock and the blessed ordinariness of that small, safe world in which we were given the time and the quiet to develop and grow sturdy. I am grateful to be reminded of a good and happy time.

London
July 1972

Joyce Grenfell

NANNY AT THE TABLE

What's for lunch, Nanny?
>A rasher of wind and a fried snowball.

What's for pudding?
>Patience pudding with wait-a-while sauce.

Fish is good for the brain.

Always eat bread with meat or you are not a
>Christian.

>Two pieces of plain bread and butter first.
>Think of all the poor starving children who'd
>be grateful for that nice plain bread and
>butter.

Eating toast crusts makes your hair curl, so eat
>them up.

>*Be sure to eat up all your boiled egg, and make a hole*
>*at the bottom of the shell so that the witches can't*
>*use it for a boat to sink the sailors' ships.*

Down the little red lane.

>This tea's too weak to crawl up the spout.
>Water bewitched and tea begrudged!

Sing at the table, die at the workhouse.

Save your breath to cool your porridge.

Never talk while eating fish or you might choke
on a bone.

Drink at the start of a meal and in between
courses, then you will avoid indigestion.

Better an empty house than a bad lodger.

No uncooked joints on the table, please.
No elbows on the table until you are an aunt.
Who's an aunt or over twenty-one?
All joints on the table shall be carved.

Always leave something for Captain Manners.
Master Manners always waits till he's asked.
*Leave something on your plate for the Duke of
Rutland's son.*

Sit up straight at the table so there's room for a
mouse at the front and a cat at the back.

If you don't behave I'll turn your back to the
table.

Stop making buttons. (Wriggling)

First come, first served.
> Those who don't ask don't get ; those who
> don't ask don't want.

What you take you eat.
Wicked waste brings woeful want.

> You've got to eat a peck of dirt before you
> die.
> Pick it up and eat it, child ; it will have lost
> nothing and gained a little.

These knives are so blunt you could ride to
> Romford on them.
> *Fingers were made before forks.*

A lady has a little of everything and then no
> more.
A piece, dear, a piece ; a bit is something that
> goes in a horse's mouth.

> May I have half a cup of tea, Nanny ?
> I don't break my cups for anyone.

Don't shovel your food , dear. You may be a
> minor, but not a miner.
> Hurry up and make a clean plate.
> If you don't eat up you'll never grow tall.

Your eyes are bigger than your stomach.
 Enough is as good as a feast.

*Thou may'st love the hooting owl but thou shouldn't love
  the roasted fowl.*

You've eaten up to dolly's wax.
You'll eat the hind leg off a donkey.
When little boys have had enough, horses are full up.

Don't take the polish off the plate.
You'll scrape the pattern off your plate.
If Greedy will wait, hot will cool.
He's not greedy but he likes a lot.

Now we're being ex and shoff. (*Excited and
  showing off*)
Too much excitement and rich food.

A little more and then no more.
Always get up from the table feeling as if you
  could still eat a penny bun.

First things first after breakfast.

NANNY ON MANNERS

Have you been?
Go out of the room and come back nicely.

A pretty face is of no use if the manners don't
 match.
Fine clothes don't make a fine lady.

You must wear clean underwear, you might get
 run over.
What shall I wear?
 Your sky blue pink.
Turn round behind and I'll do up your frock.
A lady never makes herself conspicuous by her
 hands or her feet. (*No coloured gloves or shoes*)
 Brush your hair one hundred times daily.

Now walk downstairs carefully as if you were
 dressed in china.
Be down in the hall with your gloves on and
 tuppence ready for the collection.

Horses sweat, gentlemen perspire, but ladies
 only gently glow.
Chest, not breast, dear.
 She's getting past herself.

First impressions mean a lot, so always have
    good luggage.
  Never arrive empty handed.

Always hold on to the pram while crossing the
    road.

Always hang your things up when you come in;
    the floor is the untidy man's table.
  A place for everything and everything in its place.

  Quick's the word and sharp's the toffee.
  Do it well, but it isn't church work.
Save a penny for the poorman.

  Never sit with your back to the fire.
It'll never get well if you pick it.
Don't whistle. Only stable boys do that.

  Do up your butterflies.
  Master Robert is talking German. (*Farting*)
We're not at home to Mr. Rude.

Mr. Can can't, Mr. Won't will.
  A promise is a promise and must be kept.
Consideration for other is the essence of good
    manners.
  Manners maketh man.

  Now then, behave or not at all.

NANNY AS CRITIC

There's someone not a hundred miles from here
    who's being rather stupid.

You'll sleep all your senses away.
    Rub the sleepy dust out of your eyes.

    You've got no more brains than God gave a sheep.

    Little pitchers have long ears, so have donkeys.

Very sharp we are today, we must have slept in
    the knife box.
Very sharp we are today, we must have been up
    to Sheffield.
Very sharp we are today, we'll cut ourselves if
    we're not careful.
You're so sharp you must have slept on your
    father's razor case.

    Eavesdroppers hear no good of themselves.
    Teach your grandmother to suck eggs.
    Children should be seen and not heard.

Now, don't run past yourself.

    You're not the only pebble on the beach.
    Stop blowing your own trumpet.

Self praise is no recommendation.

I thought I saw a shabby funeral going down the road. (*Boasting*)

She's a proper little madam.

Don't think yourself so pretty. Even if a man on a galloping horse did carry you off one dark night, he would drop you at the first lighted lamp post.

No one would stop a horse a-gallop to look at you.

Your hair is as straight as a yard of pump water.
It's like a furze bush in a fit.
It's been drawn through a hedge backwards.
Your hair is like heaven – there's no parting.

You look like a mud lark.
Your face is shining like Bristol beacon.
You look like a carrot half scraped.

Your vest is more holy than righteous.
Those shoes owe you no rent.

Look at your dirty finger-nails. Are we in mourning for the cat?

I want gets nothing.
Pull yourself together and pull up your socks.

Your likes and dislikes are too numerous to mention.

She'll go all round the orchard and pick a crab at
    last.
She'd bite her nose off to spite her face.

Somebody got out of bed on the wrong side this morning.

You've got the devil on your back.
There's a little black dog on your shoulder
    today.
One might as well talk to a gate post.
Who's lost his trumpeter?
Has the cat got your tongue?
I could ride to London on that lip.

A good dose of syrup is what you need.

There's more ways of killing a cat than choking
    it with cream.
I can read you like a ha'penny book with the
    leaves out.
The more you do for some people the more you
    may do.

You'll be the death of me.

Were you born in a barn?
Were you born on a raft?
Were you born in a pub with swing doors?
You make a better door than window. (*Obscuring light*)

If you play with that you'll get consumption.

No such word as 'can't'.
What do you think I am – a leaning post?
You don't want me to call you a 'cowardy-
    custard', do you?
It'll only end in tears.
Don't be a cry baby.

Fair words butter no parsnips.

All eyes and no action will get us nowhere.

If it were a dog it would have bitten you.
There's none so blind as them as won't see.
A nod's as good as a wink to a blind horse.

You could argue the hind legs off a donkey.
    You're talking double Dutch.

Little Miss Suck-a-Thumb.
Mr Nosy Parker.
    Fidgety Phil couldn't keep still.
    He's a regular little Turk.
    *You must never do that! That's what little French
       boys do.*

A second class head sticking out of a first class
      window.
    Very particular we are – it's top brick off the
      chimney or nothing.
    Her people are nobody very much.
You were good enough in the Brixton Road,
      and now you've spoilt yourself.
    Who's she? The cat's grandmother?
    That's enough to make a cat laugh.

A tom tit on a round of beef. (*Small hat*)

    That's been blown together.
    It's sewn with a hot needle and burning
      thread.
If a job is worth doing it's worth doing properly.

    He's only sixpence in the shilling, dear.

I suppose we must make the best of an indecent
      job. (*Lady defying convention*)
    What next I should like to know!

NANNY APPROVES

There's a dear smiling little kitten on your
    shoulder today.

   Well begun is half done.
   Well tried, well done.
   Some can, some can't ; some do, some don't ;
       and you're a can and do.
   What a busy bee you are.

Nobody's sweetheart is ugly.
   Blue eyes – true eyes.
   Cold hands – warm heart.
You look like Madam Rachel, beautiful for ever.

The nicest things come in the smallest parcels.
Give me a kiss and I'll give you a windmill.

   I'll rub it and kiss it well.
Here's the boy that fought the monkey in the
       dirt hole, and came out without a scratch.
   He's got all his buttons.

We didn't see anybody in the Park we liked
       better than ourselves.
   The better the day, the better the deed.

NANNY AS POET

Daniel in the den with the lions,
  Brave as a blinken span-i-el.
Dan'l didn't give a damn for the lions,
  And lions didn't care for Dan-i-el.

He who calls his brother a liar,
Shall be cast into Hell fire.

Many little cuss words, bother, dash and blow,
And other little wuss words, can send us down
      below.

Well I never, did you ever
See a monkey dressed in leather?

Be a good boy,
Do as you're bid.
Shut the door after you,
Never be chid.

When Mother calls, obey,
Do not loiter, do not stay.
    Hasten child be quick,
    Do not want another kick.

Up at eight, a well-filled plate.
Up at nine, eat with the swine.

If you in the morning throw minutes away,
    You can't make them up in the rest of the day.
You may hurry and scurry, and flurry and worry,
    You've lost them for ever and ever and aye.

First the bottom,
Then the head,
This will make a tidy bed.

The biggest doors open
To the littlest keys,
'Yes, thank you' and 'If you please'.

The little boy who would not say 'Thank you'
    and 'If you please',
Was scraped to death with oyster shells
    among the Caribbees.

Don't care was made to care; don't care was
    hung.
Don't care was put in a pot and boiled till he
    was done.

Good, better, best,
Never let it rest,
Till your good is better
And you better, best.

Evening grey and morning red,
The lamb and ewe go wet to bed.

Good-night, sleep tight, mind the fleas don't
    bite.
If they do, get a shoe and crack their little heads
    in two.

One, two, three, Mother caught a flea,
    Put it in a tea cup and made a cup of tea.
When she put the milk in it rose to the top,
    When she put the sugar in, it went off pop.

Last Sunday morning we missed him from the mat,
Puss, puss, puss, meat, meat, meat.
    Has anybody seen our cat?

It is a sin to steal a pin.
Much more to steal a bigger thing.

See a pin and pick it up,
    All day long you'll have good luck.
See a pin and let it lie,
    You'll have bad luck until you die.

If you have a ring above the nose,
You'll never wear your wedding clothes.

Make new friends, but keep the old,
The one is silver, the other gold.

Man is born to pain and trouble,
Both in single and in double.

Along comes Nanny with a red hot poultice,
  Claps it on and takes no notice.
'Oh,' says the doctor, 'that's much too hot.'
  'Oh no,' says Nanny, 'I'm sure it's not.'

It's a dog's delight to bark and bite – not that of
    little girls.

We don't like that girl from Tooting Bec,
She washes her face, and forgets her neck.

Patience is a virtue, virtue is a grace,
Put them both together and you get a pretty
    face.

Little girl:
Box of paints:
Sucked her brush:
Joined the saints.

Curiosity killed the cat,
Information made it fat.

Curiosity killed the cat,
Generosity brought it back.

If ifs and ands were pots and pans,
there'd be no room for tinkers.

Brown and blue will never do.
Pink makes the boys wink.

Tinker, tailor, soldier and a sailor,
All waiting at the old barn door.
What the dick, dick, dickens are they waiting
for?
Perhaps to see the cheese made? No!
Perhaps to see the butter made? No!
Perhaps to see the milkmaid? Aha ha!

Tom Thumper;
Bill Milker;
Long Lacee;
Cherry Bumper;
And the little old man who wouldn't get over
the stile.

Baby-bye, here's a fly,
Let us catch him, you and I.
There he goes, on his toes,
Tickling Baby's nose.

Ha, ha, ha, hee, hee, hee, cat's in the cupboard -
and he can't catch me.

NANNY AS PHILOSOPHER

Teach your head to save your heels.
 More haste, less speed.

'How time flies,' said the monkey, as he threw
 the clock out of the window.

 A stitch in time saves nine.
 You can always make time.
 Never put off till tomorrow what you can do today.

Cheer up for Chatham! Dover's in sight.
The longest way round is the shortest way
 home.
If you go by the road of Bye and Bye you'll
 never arrive.

 One leg at a time, as lawyers go to heaven.

Now I must get on, this will never get the baby
 a new coat.
 I'm coming – so's Christmas.

There's another day tomorrow.
 All being spared and well.

You'll enjoy it when you get there.

You are full of small complaints no baby dies
of.

Don't worry it will all come out in the wash.
Cleanliness is next to Godliness.
Go upstairs and wash your face and hands and
you'll feel better.

Worse things happen at sea.

You must suffer in order to be beautiful.
Handsome is as handsome does.

Well, you're not backward in coming
forward.
Laugh before seven, cry before eleven.

She's going through a phrase.

Stir the pot with a long spoon to let the devil
come out of the steam.
Messrs Salts and Senna and Doctor Greenfield
will soon put you right.
That's good riddance to bad rubbish.

Help yourself and your friends will love you.
    The Lord will provide, dear, but you must
        give him some help.

    You can't have the penny and the bun.

Never mind if you don't win so long as you did
        your best; someone has to lose.
    Bad workmen blame their tools.

It's six of one and half a dozen of the other.

Nothing falls off except buttons.

Just because he puts his head in the fire, there's
        no reason for you to.
    Never trouble trouble till trouble troubles you.

    Remember the two nice bears, bear and
        forbear.
Little birds in their nests must agree and not fall
    out.

Sticks and stones may break my bones but hard
        words cannot hurt me.

    Never let the sun go down on your anger.
    If you never raise your voice in anger, you
        will rarely need to raise your hand.

When you can step on six daisies at once,
summer has come.

Thunder is clouds knocking together.

Wasps only upset you if you upset them.

If there's enough blue sky to make a pair of
sailor's trousers then you can go out.

You'll never miss the water till the well runs
dry.

All in a line like old Brown's cows.

Put salt on its tail.

Now that's an idea – but not a very good one.

We shall see what we shall see.

If wishes were horses, beggars would ride.

You never know your luck till your number
turns up.

Tell the truth and shame the devil.

When God shuts a door he always opens a
window.

Clear as you go and you won't be in a muddle.

A little praise works better than a lot of
nagging.

NANNY AT BEDTIME

Skin a rabbit!

Put your dressing-gown on, darling; it's rude to
     be naked.
Don't tie your pyjama cord so tightly.
     Remember one swells in the night.

Milk of magnesia cools the blood.

What a face to go to bed with.
All you need is a night between the sheets to put
     you right.

A dry bed deserves a boiled sweet.

Up the wooden hill to Bedfordshire.
     Come on, up wooden hill, down sheet lane.

Sleep before midnight is beauty sleep.
The longer you sleep, the longer you'll grow.

Here's beds for sleepyheads.
Watch for the sandman.
Close your eyes because the sandman is coming.

Sleep tight, wake bright.

NANNY

Virginia Graham

Where is my Nanny in her long grey coat and skirt,
    and a black straw hat stuck with a pin to her head?
Where has she gone with her creaking petersham belt,
    and the strange, flat, comforting, senseless things she
        said?

'Cheer up, chicken, you'll soon be hatched!' she would
        tell me,
    drying my ears in a rough methodical way,
and 'Mark my words, it'll come out in the wash',
    and 'It's just Sir Garnet Wolseley!' she used to say.

I still don't know what she meant, but oh, it was nice
    to hear that distrait voice so ruggedly tender,
as glimmering starchily she would cross the room
    to hang my liberty bodice on the fender.

Would she were here on this perilous bomb-scarred
        night,
    as warm and satisfying as a loaf of bread,
to stand like a round shield between me and the world,
    to give me a bath and carry me up to bed.

(1944)